Once Upon a Coc[...] the County of Lo[s ...] ancestral and unceded [homelands of the] Tongva, Tataviam, Serrano, Kizh, and Chumash Peoples, a land once known as Tovaangar (which includes hundreds of square miles of the Los Angeles Basin), and that is still home to many Gabrieleño Tongva. **We honor and pay respect to their elders and** descendants - past, present, and emerging. We recognize and are grateful their vital stewardship of this land continues into our future.

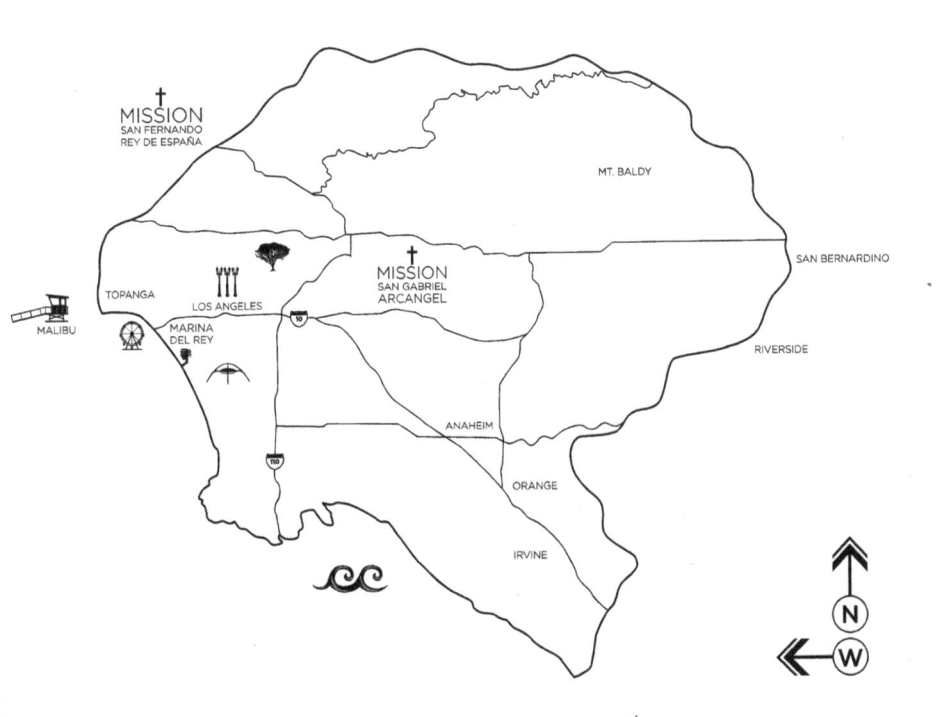

THIS BOOK IS DEDICATED TO DIVINE TIMING!

© 2024 Welcome to the Brightside™. All rights reserved.

First Edition ISBN PRINT: 979-8-218-98767-1
First Edition ISBN E-BOOK: 979-8-218-98768-8

Library of Congress Control Number: 2024922774

No portion of this book may be reproduced in any fashion, print, scanned, facsimile, or electronic format, or by any method yet to be developed, without express written permission from the artist and author.

Katie Brightside has asserted her moral rights under the Copyright, Designs and Patents Act to be identified as the author of this work. All artwork and pages are illustrated by Welcome to the Brightside™ and set in Gotham* and the original hand-crafted font, Brightside Fairytale**.

Author, illustrations, book cover design, & graphic design: Katie Brightside
Cocktail Contributor: Sarah L.M. Mengoni
Editor: K Ryan Henisey

Publisher: Welcome to the Brightside
Printed and bound in the United States of America

The typeface Gotham* is licensed from Monotype.

In 1807, amongst an elite group of writers, New York City received the nickname Gotham. The word derives from a medieval English word Gottam which literally means Goat Home. The name caught on as a colloquialism, in the press and on buildings.

*The typeface Gotham is named after the urban landscape that inspired it, New York. Designed by Jonathan Hoefler and Tobias Frere-Jones in 2000 for GQ Magazine. The font was included in the MoMA permanent collection in 2011.

**The Brightside Fairytale font was created by Welcome to the Brightside™ in 2017 for the book A Modern Moral, a series of original, commissioned artworks and revised fairytales.

onceuponacocktail.world

Once upon a Cocktail™

LOS ANGELES

THE LA GUIDE TO THE NON-ALCOHOLIC MOVEMENT!

**WRITTEN & ILLUSTRATED BY
KATIE BRIGHTSIDE**

WITH SARAH L.M. MENGONI

—

Welcome to the Brightside™

West Hollywood, California

ONCE UPON A COCKTAIL

A huge THANK YOU to everyone listed on this page. Without your support, this book would not have been possible.

Jessica Agapetus, Kirsty Ainsworth, Laurel Alexander, Lisa Alexander, Anonymous, Carly Blessing, Ian Blessing, LP O'Brien, Carol Bright, Derek Brown, Bryan Bruce, Mike Capoferri, Rachel Champlin, Jamie Chilberg, Becky Crawley, Ashley Darar, Lisa DeMartino, Arleo De Guzman, Morris Ellis, Essie Evans, Sarah Fagundez, Antonia Fattizzi, James Frankie, Brianda Gonzalez, Douglas Hahn, Jordan Haskell, K. Ryan Henisey, Dan Hodgdon, Matt Johns, Lisa King, Theo Kinman, Katie Kosyan, Shirelle LaTortue, Aaron Leopold, Tom Liu, Stacey Mann, Rachel Miller, Arnold Mina, Joseph Mintz, Pablo Murillo, Brian Niermeyer, Bryant J. Orozco, Lori Pedrick, Amber Pennington, Corey Phillips, Summer Phoenix, Josh Pritchard, Samantha Savary, Naomi Schimek, Daryl Schwartz, Megan Shepherd, Natalie Silbar, Brynn Smith, Shana Wong Solares, Jon Spacher, Randy Tarlow, Michael Tebbe, Amanda Victoria, Rey III Viquez and Cherilyn Wilson.

To all *Once Upon a Cocktail* partners and sponsors, thank you all.

drink@onceuponacocktail.world

TABLE OF CONTENTS

1   Land Acknowledgment
4   Thank You's

6   Foreword | **LP O'Brien**
9   Recipe | **LP O'Brien**

12   Introduction

14   Anonymous | **Plaid Circus**

18   Derek Brown | **Positive Damage** | **Stay Zero Proof**

20   Bryan Bruce | **The Overland**

22   Morris Ellis, Pablo Murillo & Bryant J. Orozco | **Bar Nuda**

24   Essie Evans | **Shirley's Temple**

26   Brianda Gonzalez | **The New Bar**

30   Arleo De Guzman & Amber Pennington | **Free Spirited**

32   Tom Liu | **Thunderbolt**

34   Corey Phillips | **Kimpton Everly Hotel**

36   Naomi Schimek | **Schimek Studios**

38   Daryl Schwartz | **Good + Bar**

40   Brynn Smith | **Bar Next Door**

42   Preparation Recipes
48   Afterword

LP O'BRIEN | FOREWORD

I'm LP O'Brien, a mixologist, beverage consultant, and winner of Netflix's "Drink Masters." My passion for pushing the boundaries of drink culture has been the driving force behind my journey through the world of beverages. From cozy, tucked-away bars in small towns to dazzling events in bustling global cities, I've always aimed to craft drinks that go beyond the ordinary. Whether it's an elegant cocktail or a refreshing non-alcoholic creation, my mission is to create memorable moments that linger in the mind and on the palate. Every sip should evoke something meaningful, whether it's a sense of comfort, nostalgia, or excitement for something new.

The world of beverages is vast and ever-evolving, and along the way, I've had the privilege of collaborating with some of the brightest minds and most forward-thinking brands in the industry. Through my travels and experiences, I've witnessed firsthand the incredible shift towards more inclusive, spirit-free options that reflect a more mindful approach to drinking. This movement toward non-alcoholic (NA) beverages is no longer just a niche interest—it's a cultural phenomenon that is reshaping how we all think about what it means to enjoy a drink. My involvement in this movement started years ago, and for me, it's been more than just a professional endeavor. It's a personal mission to help people see that they don't have to choose between enjoyment and mindfulness—they can have both.

@lpdrinksdc

My connection with Sarah L.M. Mengoni goes way back to a Kimpton Hotels Beverage Summit, where we first crossed paths, united by a shared passion for reimagining drinks without alcohol. Our relationship quickly blossomed into a deep friendship built on mutual respect and a desire to push the industry forward. Watching Mengoni evolve into a true trailblazer in the NA space has been nothing short of inspiring. She's someone who sees beyond trends and taps into the core of what people really want—connection, experience, and enjoyment without compromise. Our mutual commitment to the NA movement has only deepened over time, and I am constantly inspired by her dedication to redefining how people think about drinking. Together with Katie Brightside, the vision for this book is the culmination of years of hard work, innovation, and an unwavering love for the craft.

The NA movement isn't just about removing alcohol—it's about so much more. It's about building community, giving people choices, and celebrating the art of drink-making in a way that speaks to everyone, regardless of whether or not they choose to consume alcohol. I've seen this movement spread like wildfire, from the heart of Los Angeles to vibrant cities across Europe, Asia, and beyond. Each city and culture adds its own unique flair to the movement, but the underlying message is universal: inclusion and mindfulness are here to stay. I still remember an event in London where spirit-free drinks were just as sought after as the classics, proving that this movement isn't just a trend—it's a cultural revolution. People everywhere are embracing the idea that you can have a beautifully crafted, flavorful drink without the alcohol, and they're hungry for more.

Looking ahead, I have no doubt that the NA movement will continue to thrive and grow, fueled by the creativity and passion of pioneers like Brightside and Mengoni. This book captures a pivotal moment in that journey, spotlighting the trailblazers who are reshaping the industry and opening doors to new possibilities. It's a testament to the power of innovation and the impact that a single idea can have when it resonates with so many.

Once Upon a Cocktail isn't just another guide to non-alcoholic drinks—it's a manifesto for the future of cocktail culture. Brightside and Mengoni have tapped into the pulse of the NA movement at just the right time, offering insights, stories, and connections that make this book a must-read for anyone curious about the growing world of alcohol-free beverages. They've crafted a resource that will not only educate but inspire readers to explore a new world of flavor and possibility.

Packed with stories of the movement's pioneers and brimming with inspiration, this guide will do more than educate—it will empower a new generation of mindful drinkers. It will encourage them to think differently about what they're drinking and why, and to see the possibilities in every glass, whether it contains alcohol or not. I'm honored to write this foreword because I believe wholeheartedly in the vision Brightside and Mengoni have brought to life. Their work will shape the future of drinking, one thoughtful sip at a time, and I can't wait to see the ripple effects that this book will have across the world.

So, whether you're a seasoned beverage professional or someone just beginning to explore the world of non-alcoholic drinks, *Once Upon a Cocktail - Los Angeles, Non-Alcoholic Movement* is your invitation to join this exciting movement. The future of drink culture is bright, inclusive, and filled with possibility—and this book is your guide to it all.

Siponey Spritz Co. makes premium award-winning fizzy and refreshing cocktails using real ingredients. In 2022, LP O'Brien joined the team as a shareholder following her historic win of Netflix's reality cocktail show, "Drink Masters." Siponey Spritz Co. commits two percent of revenues annually to non-profit environmental organizations around the world and is dedicated to saving honeybees, one can at a time.

@ siponeyspritzco

VIBRANTE SPRITZ

Build in a footed tulip glass filled with ice.

2 oz Martini and Rossi Vibrante N/A Aperitivo
4 oz Fever-Tree Pink Grapefruit Soda

Moisten one side of the rim of the glass
with a grapefruit wheel and coat with pulverized kosher salt.
Garnish with a half-moon of grapefruit.

Siponey

POLLINATOR
Our Play on a Smash

hibiscus, berries, lemon & a touch of organic honey

12 FL OZ (355 ML)

BOTANICS
Our Play on a Paloma

grapefruit, key lime, rosemary & a touch of organic honey

12 FL OZ (355 ML)

TROPICS
Our Play on a Punch

pineapple, key lime, cinnamon & a touch of organic honey

12 FL OZ (355 ML)

ROOTS
Our Play on a Mule

ginger, key lime, turmeric & a touch of organic honey

12 FL OZ (355 ML)

Enjoy Alone or Add Your Favorite Spirit

Non-Alcoholic Cocktails

1% FOR THE PLANET · MADE WITH ALL REAL INGREDIENTS · Certified B Corporation

siponey.com

FEVER-TREE®

IF 3/4 OF
YOUR DRINK
IS THE MIXER,
MIX WITH
THE BEST.

INTRODUCTON

Welcome to the *Once Upon a Cocktail – West Hollywood's* (WeHo) addendum. This addition was inspired by the research for a TV appearance. Due to the program's "no alcohol" rule, we were asked to make recipes from the WeHo book non-alcoholic. The reception of this segment was so well received, it laid the groundwork for who we would come to showcase in *Once Upon a Cocktail - The LA Guide to the Non-Alcoholic Movement!*

Why was there a need to adapt the recipes for the TV show? During research and development (R&D) for WeHo in 2022, there was one non-alcoholic cocktail in the city that shined enough to land coverage on a page. Timing is everything and during the recovery landscape from the most isolating period of our lives, most of the products and brands we see on our shelves were still in their infancy or being cooked up in home kitchens. Now, the alcohol-free sector is a rapidly growing space in the spirit industry—we use the word "spirit" loosely as it nuzzles its way into that category, even though it's zero proof!

From this point forward we will refer to "Non-Alcoholic" as NA and "Alcohol-Free" as AF. As this is an addendum we have no glossary, glassware, tool guide, or cocktail terms and techniques. If you need guidance for recipes, please refer to the WeHo book. From a design perspective, this book is illustrated with portraits of the interviewed subjects as stylized black and white vector drawings,

@onceuponacocktail.world

or as Naomi Schimek quipped, "now I magically turn into a Patrick Nagel girl." We went bold to identify the chapters with a strong use of color, which in turn relates to the color in the Table of Contents and title of method in Preparation Recipes on page 42.

Instead of historical nuggets like WeHo, this book presents twelve curated snapshots of differing perspectives in the NA movement. This is a guidebook to Los Angeles County's diverse players in this movement and their key position shaping it.

The not-so-dirty dozen have shared their beloved NA recipes, and we are grateful to them and the legendary LP O'Brien for their generous contributions.

Our line up starts with Anonymous, whose secret identity will never be revealed. Their partnership with Plaid Circus is an exciting discovery and we are honored that a brand took a risk to showcase their future world-class product. Stay Zero Proof's beverage director Derek Brown is a leader in the AF space. With a few books under his belt, it's been a privilege to have his contribution to this book. The Overland's boundary breaking Bryan Bruce uses spirits as both ingredients and reimagines them into syrups. A homage to heritage comes from the three amigos at Bar Nuda. Essie Evans' Shirley's Temple was LA's first ever NA bar. Brianda Gonzalez's shares a successful navigation from a negative experience into a positive with a NA store and strong brand identity. Free Spirited contributes their own resourceful in-house spirits. The award-winning Thunderbolt has a recipe so good they are re-working a version with liquor. Representing the corporate hotel world, Corey Phillips makes a bold statement with twenty-five percent of his menu AF drinks. Naomi Schimek adds an elegant approach using tea. The journey of Good + Bar founder Daryl Schwartz and his functional cocktails imprint change on the activation and event space. And Brynn Smith of Bar Next Door executes the classics as zero-proof.

This new category has been captivating to investigate and compile into a bite-size collection. Most of all, it has been inspirational to collaborate with so many dream-makers and AF evangelists. Thank you all for sharing your stories and vision.

Dear reader, please enjoy these pages and know that love created it. Bottoms up!

ANONYMOUS | PLAID CIRCUS

The Banksy of the mixology world, Anonymous (Anon), is a Californian native and an LA bartending shake queen! One step ahead of the spirit-free sector, Anon has partnered with Plaid Circus, a shiny-new brand in the zero-proof market.

Plaid Circus is the creation of a dynamic duo; entrepreneur Daniel Hodgdon, and a recovering advertiser Brian Niermeyer, who quit his day job to turn his homemade moonshine into his dream!

"Geographically, this is an LA movement," notes liquor industry veteran Anon, "it is happening here first and then will have a ripple effect out to the rest of the world"

"Several years ago, the industry didn't think the NA movement had traction. With skyrocketing prices, people drinking less, younger demographics who have a health-conscious perspective, and evolving laws on cannabis have led to a general reset of habits. I predict the NA movement is going to explode and we're just scratching the surface of where this may lead."

"Plaid Circus, by far, has created the best NA products to hit the market," continues Anon, "all their ingredients are organic, no additives, no coloring, and no artificial flavoring. There are a couple of unique flavors like Bubblegum Fantasy and Tangerine Dream, as well as more classic profiles such as the bourbon-forward flavor called Plaidhattan, which has a subtle burn on the back of your throat. All the flavors are robust, real, and bold. From my twenty years of experience, I suggest putting your money on Plaid Circus as a brand to watch."

plaidcircus.com

WELCOME TO THE CIRCUS

Serve in a chilled flute. Shake with ice and strain. Top with soda.

1.5 oz Plaid Circus Bubblegum Fantasy
0.5 oz fresh lemon juice
0.25 oz Liquid Alchemist Orgeat Syrup
2.5 oz Fever-Tree Sparkling Pink Grapefruit Soda

Moisten half the rim of the glass with a lemon wheel and coat with a mix of edible pink glitter, salt, and sugar. Express oils from a lemon peel over the cocktail and rub onto the side of the glass. Garnish with baby's breath attached by a mini clothespin**.

**Baby's breath is not an edible flower and may cause stomach upset if consumed.

PLAID CIRCUS

FOR WHEN YOU'VE OUTGROWN ALCOHOL.

PC

HAND CRAFTED IN DANVILLE, KY

DISCOVER MORE FLAVORS.

Life is Short... Drink Great Cocktails

LIQUID ALCHEMIST

PREMIUM COCKTAIL SYRUPS

Liquid-Alchemist.com

DEREK BROWN | STAY ZERO PROOF

Derek Brown is the founder of Positive Damage, co-founder of Mindful Drinking Fest, and cocktail consultant for Chinatown's first NA venue, Stay Zero Proof.

Stay was in the former Hong Kong Café, which was at the epicenter of LA's Punk scene—along with neighboring Chinese restaurant rival Madame Wong's. This boundary-pushing venue gave meaning to Punk's anti-establishment. Going against the grain, Stay was the embodiment of progressive futurists.

"Stacey Mann and Summer Phoenix approached me last year about opening Stay after Stacey Googled 'best zero-proof mixologist.' She reached out and I just happened to have my laptop open. So, I replied immediately. Whether or not I'm the 'best zero-proof mixologist' is up for debate, but Bon Appétit did call me a 'non-alcoholic mixology wizard,' so I'll take it."

Stay sadly shut its doors in September 2024. "Obviously, it's a blow to me and the owners, but it was also a space ahead of its time. Sometimes when you swing big, you miss. But they created something so special and incredible that it's bound to live on in the people who visited—and in the pages of this book."

To Stacey and Summer, if you are reading this, we are deeply sorry for the loss of Stay. Thank you for creating a place we will never forget!

@positivedamageinc

THE TIGER

Serve in a coupe. Shake with ice and strain.

1.5 oz Free Spirits Tequila
1 oz lapsang souchong tea
0.75 oz agave syrup*
1 oz fresh pineapple juice
1 oz fresh lime juice
1 dash Tabasco Green Jalapeno Sauce
1 dash salt tincture*

Moisten half the rim of the glass with a lime wheel and coat with tajin.

*See page 42 Preparation Recipes.

BRYAN BRUCE | THE OVERLAND

We were pleased to meet Bryan Bruce, the owner-operator of The Overland, in Redlands, California. We are highly aware this bar is not within LA County lines but we think what Bruce is showcasing on his drink menu is worth hopping counties.

With an eye for detail, Bruce has designed and curated every inch of The Overland, from the interiors and music to the menus. With over 2,000 records from Bruce's personal collection, the bar's "bring your own vinyl" all day Happy-Hour is a local favorite.

With twenty percent of the menu carefully geared towards NA drinks, Bruce believes inclusivity is vital.

When asked about the movement, he was pleased to share the wonderful innovations he's made in this new category of cocktails. "I take these non-alcoholic spirits, use them as they are in NA cocktails, and turn them into syrups for both NA and alcoholic cocktails. This category continues to spur creativity in all areas, while not taking away from the experience of people who cannot drink it. At this moment, the movement is a large focal point in the spirit industry and NA options are becoming more thoughtful. I am not entirely sure where the future of it will go but I really like the idea that brands and people are making these new flavors, as opposed to just the one style of something to sip."

@the_overland_bar

QUEEN'S HIGHWAY

Serve in a rocks glass. Shake with ice and strain.

1.5 oz Ritual Zero Proof Tequila Alternative
0.5 oz beet syrup*
0.5 oz pineapple syrup*
1 oz fresh orange juice
1 tsp citric acid solution*

Garnish with a half-moon of orange.

*See page 42 Preparation Recipes.

ELLIS, MURILLO & OROZCO | BAR NUDA

"I believe the NA space is a movement as opposed to a moment. I don't think it's going anywhere," champions Pablo Murillo.

The three amigos of the Mexican inspired, NA, pop-up Bar Nuda, as illustrated, Morris Ellis (left), Murillo (center) and mixologist Bryant J. Orozco (right). Ellis and Murillo formed Aguas Locas, a Latin beverage company. Through this endeavor they met spirit aficionado and herbalist Orozco.

Every quarter, Orozco hops the border with a suitcase full of authentically sourced ingredients. Ellis states, "we're not just creating an NA Margarita or Old-Fashion; we are turning back to our heritage to make new versions of beverages."

"Latinos were not introduced to distilled spirits until they were colonized," continues Murillo. Before then we drank aguas frescas, tepache and pulque. Those were made illegal to produce and sell after colonization. At Bar Nuda we are taking that back, remaking drinks, and reusing ingredients."

"Bar Nuda, in Spanish translates to nude or bare," expresses Ellis. Conceptually, he means "without alcohol we are exposed, our vulnerable selves in our bare state. We are not masked by booze. We want everyone to come to a Bar Nuda event or pop-up as themselves to form genuine connections."

"'Drink to Remember' is our slogan. We want to make having good times without alcohol easier, to enjoy the social ritual and the belly laughs," states Murillo.

@barnuda.la

MARIPOSA

Build in collins glass filled with ice. Top with soda water.

1.5 oz Ritual Zero Proof Gin Alternative
1 oz Butterfly Pea Flower and Menta Blanca Syrup
Splash of citrus (lime or lemon)
Fever-Tree Soda Water

Garnish with Thai basil blossom.

Butterfly Pea Flower Menta Blanca Syrup
Good for two weeks in the fridge, enough for seven servings.
Add six butterfly pea flowers to 8 oz of boil-hot water; steep three minutes,
then strain. Add 1 tsp menta blanca (or dried peppermint); steep seven minutes.
Measure the liquid and add an equal amount of granulated sugar.
Stir until dissolved.

ESSIE EVANS | SHIRLEY'S TEMPLE

Imagine the entire Beehive, dressed up in glitter cowboy hats attending a 'Cowboy Carter' album drop party. Everyone sang their favorite karaoke Queen Bey song and eventually the crowd belted together. "That was one of the most memorable events," expressed Essie Evans, the owner of LA County's first ever NA bar, Shirley's Temple.

Flying solo, Evans took a risk and poured her entire life savings into a dream. Motivated by her family's turbulent relationship with drugs and alcohol, Evan's created a safe space for a growing community.

"I didn't just go into this blindly," she expressed, but despite having a strong corporate resume in the food and beverage industry, "the money ran dry." Shirley's Temple shut down a little after a year in operation, September 2024.

"The NA movement is relatively niche but maybe, in the next three years, it will normalize, and people can stay afloat. I'll go back to work in HR, but I would still love to circle back at some point." Whatever chapter is next for Essie Evans, we know it's brave to follow a dream. She is a renegade leader who pushes boundaries and takes fearless chances!

@shesnotshirley

MANGO'S MUSE

Build in a rocks glass filled with ice.

**1 oz Trejo's Spirits Tequila Alternative
1.5 oz Portland Mango Habanero Syrup
Dash of lime
4 oz Fever-Tree Soda Water**

Moisten the rim of the glass with a lime wheel and coat with tajin. Garnish with a cayenne pepper and fresh mint.

BRIANDA GONZALEZ | THE NEW BAR

Brianda Gonzalez is the founder and CEO of The New Bar, with three locations in California. "My family immigrated from Mexico to the US when I was seven," begins Gonzalez, "and we began our new life on Catalina Island. The island's economy is driven by hospitality and food and beverage. My father was a bartender, and I have worked in restaurants since I was twelve and became a cocktail waitress at eighteen. After my dad was diagnosed with an autoimmune illness, I looked for a way that we could practice mixology together without damaging his health. In 2020, I became obsessed with the entire alcohol-free space. Originally The New Bar was an online concept to curate, source and vet the best NA products from all over the world."

A graduate of UCLA in economics and entrepreneurship, Gonzalez began her career with tech start-ups and go-to-market strategy, working on partnership marketing and business development. Gonzalez quit her job in 2022 to pivot permanently and open the Venice store. "The knowledge from the tech job fed into The New Bar, especially as brand partners are key for the store and pop-ups, events and festivals, such as Coachella and Stagecoach. Within these front facing opportunities, there is strong interest from consumers to discover the category," expresses Gonzalez.

The New Bar has evolved through incredible branding to encourage curiosity in anyone who wants to learn about the personally curated product Gonzalez showcases both online and in store.

@thenewbar

THE NEW BAR MARGARITA

Serve in a rocks glass filled with ice.
Shake with one ice cube for eight seconds then strain.

3 oz Almave Blanco
0.25 oz Hagave Spiced Nectar
0.25 oz agave syrup*
0.5 oz fresh lime juice
3 dashes All The Bitter Orange Bitters

Moisten the rim of the glass with a lime wheel and coat with citrus salt*.
Garnish with a habanero pepper and a dehydrated lime wheel.

*See page 42 Preparation Recipes.

THE NEW BAR

Alcohol-free Drinks

Discover the best nonalcoholic wines, beers, and spirits from all over the world.

- FEMALE FOUNDED
- POST-ALC SINCE '22
- TASTE TESTED & CURATED
- VENICE, WEHO, SF

Shop at one of our stores in Venice + West Hollywood + San Francisco or online at thenewbar.com

@thenewbar

Join our newsletter!

ALL THE BITTER

BITTERS MADE **BETTER.**

Handmade in small batches

Organic herbs and adaptogens

May support gut and liver health

No added extracts, flavors, or colors

Trusted by top bartenders

0% ABV
For drinks with or without alcohol

Featured in the New York Times, Washington Post, Forbes, Food Network

PENNINGTON & DE GUZMAN | FREE SPIRITED

"Sober isn't a dirty word, you're just trying to be better for yourself," states Amber Pennington.

The happy ending of a fairy tale offers hope that good always triumphs over evil. The evil in this story is Pennington being left for dead in a drunk-driving accident. The perpetrator was sentenced to nine years in prison for aggravated hit and run, resulting in serious bodily injury.

Despite a family warning that alcohol can be addictive, Arleo De Guzman overindulged, which resulted in a sobering DUI.

These two events resulted in a serendipitous meeting of two hearts. "It was a mutual friend's birthday, and we caught each other's eye," expresses Pennington.

De Guzman, a graduate from USC in biochemistry, is a career bartender. Sommelier Pennington has vast experience in Michelin star restaurants. Together they created and opened Free Spirited on the anniversary of the day they met.

At Free Spirited everything is done in-house. Together they have crafted and developed recipes to make their own spirits using reduction techniques and fresh ingredients from discarded parts of fruits and vegetables. This also keeps their cocktails at a low price point, which always includes tax and tip.

Every cocktail has a narrative that would make any romantic melt. This is a love story that grew out of extraordinary trials and tribulations and Free Spirited is the result of that!

@free.spirited.lounge

BELAROSA

Serve in a hurricane glass with ice. Shake with ice and strain.

2.5 oz aloe herb spirit*
0.5 oz demerara syrup*
1 oz blackberry balsamic shrub*
1 oz acidified grapefruit juice*

Garnish with a blackberry and fresh mint.

*See page 42 Preparation Recipes.

The Belarosa is a mash up of both Pennington & De Guzman's family names. It's also the last name of their baby, due early 2025, swoon!

TOM LIU | THUNDERBOLT

Warning! The drinks at Thunderbolt will astonish.

Temple Street, in Historic Filipinotown, is home to Thunderbolt. Since opening in September 2019, the venue has endured a rollercoaster ride. With not enough time to iron the kinks before lockdown, continual pivoting was key. Still, it secured an eighth place in 2024's North America's 50 Best Bars List with a further accolade of 'Best in the West USA.'

Mike Capoferri and his team have built a neighborhood cocktail bar with world class drinks. We were lucky to wrangle an interview with head bartender Tom Liu. Liu noted on his travels "there is a trend for speed, consistency and zero pompousness and Thunderbolt is aligned with that trend."

Thunderbolt with its forward-thinking, tech-savvy, cocktail program has two stellar NA drinks to pick from: the Lychee Daiquiri and The Pride of Oxnard. The latter was inspired by local Strawberry production, takes two days to prepare, seconds to serve and uses 'angry bubbles,' aka forced carbonation. During the pivot of lockdown, Thunderbolt became a leader in fresh-to-customer, sparkling canned cocktails. Liu noted that the Lychee Daiquiri is so good "as soon as my boss nailed the recipe, we agreed we need to figure out the alcohol version."

@thunderboltla

LYCHEE DAIQUIRI

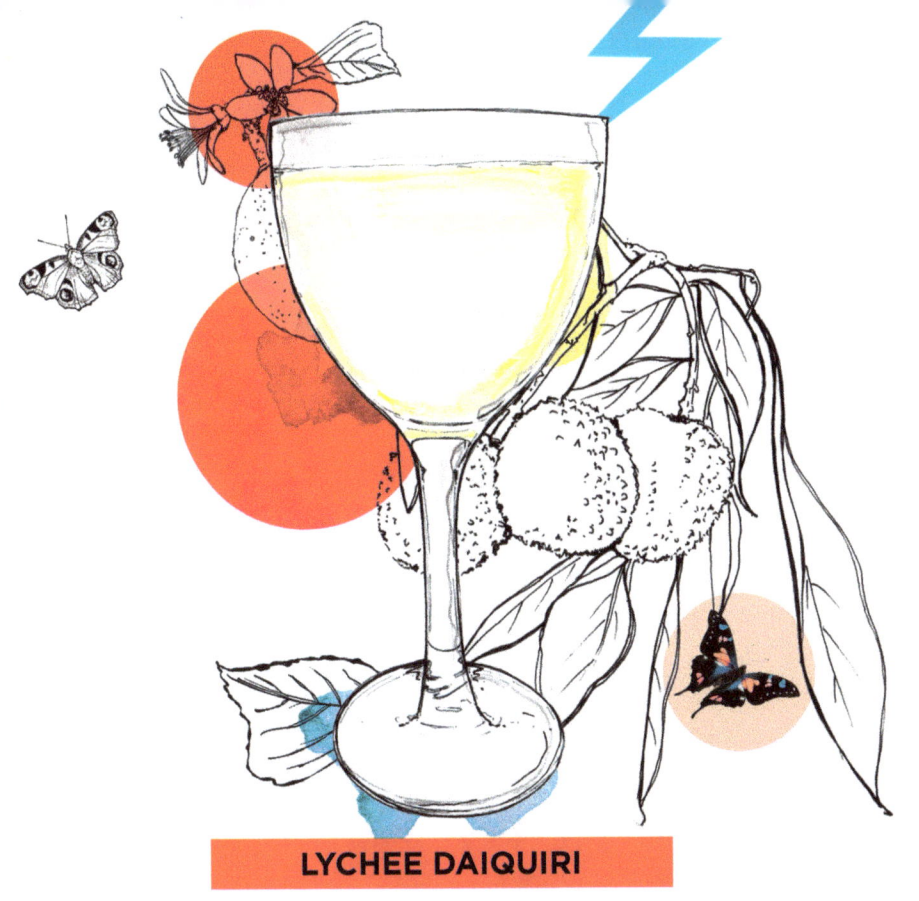

Serve in a chilled nick and nora glass. Shake with ice and strain.

2.5 oz Lychee Daiquiri Base
0.75 oz fresh lime juice
2 drops salt tincture*

Lychee Daiquiri Base
(Good for four days in the fridge, enough for eight cocktails)
Put one can (20 oz) of peeled, pitted lychee and syrup in a blender and puree until the mix is smooth, without any lumps. Whisk in 0.75 tsp glycerin with 0.75 tsp OliveNation Rum Emulsion.

*See page 42 Preparation Recipes.

COREY PHILLIPS | EVERLY HOTEL

Corey Phillips is food and beverage director of the Everly Hotel in Hollywood. During his tenure, Phillips has implemented changes to rebuild the entire team. One of his key players on the current beverage program is *Once Upon a Cocktail's* Sarah L.M. Mengoni—yes, our cocktail shaker queen is working together with this NA innovator. Utilizing all the beautiful ingredient options that California has to offer, Phillips is the driving force behind making twenty-five percent of the Everly's cocktail menu alcohol-free. This is a bold move for a hotel.

"The movement is really blowing up and I think that we're able to make a statement here at the Everly. When I go out to a bar or a restaurant, it is tiresome having limited NA choices." "Phillips, five years alcohol-free, wanted, "a program that makes you feel like even though you don't drink or you're pregnant, everyone is catered for and included with enough options that you can still feel like you're participating socially."

It is true artistry when you can imprint your life experiences on your work manifesto. Phillips' NA program is one to watch as it shakes up the LA scene.

@everlyhollywood

ESPRESSO REFRESHER

Build in a collins glass then fill with ice.

1.5 oz DrZeroZero AmarNo
2 oz espresso
0.25 oz Liquid Alchemist Passion Fruit Syrup
2 oz fresh orange juice
1 oz Fever-Tree Soda Water

Garnish with a sprig of thyme attached by mini clothespin.

NAOMI SCHIMEK | SCHIMEK STUDIOS

Naomi Schimek, a theater major at Santa Monica College, spent most of her adult life on the West Coast. Schimek considers bartending her stage, stating, "I have used that performative education my entire career, whether behind the bar, as a brand ambassador, or speaking to a crowd."

"I've worked the gamut," explains Schimek, "dive bars, restaurants, fine dining, and clubs. My ideal setting is an eight-twelve seat omakase-style place. However, I find myself mostly employed at venues with volume service." An avid forager with a green finger and sense for fresh, local ingredients to inspire her craft, Schimek's earthy approach juxtaposes audacious and simplistic flavors. Her unwavering talent has gained recognition for Spare Room and Soulmate. Now in the LA Kimpton fold, she will be an asset to evolve the cocktail program to a heightened elegance!

"Whether utilizing pastry techniques or foraging for California native plants, dynamic garnishes interest me," explains Schimek on honing her culinary craft and looking forward to further education in pastry.

"Everybody feels fancier with a gorgeous drink in their hands," comments Schimek on the evolving growth of the NA movement and its emphasis on inclusivity. "I think brands have their place and are important. However, there are several reasons I like creating my own flavor combinations and extracts; pairing herbs or using teas to discover intricate and nuanced pairings. Why use a brand when there is such a wild library of flavors to paint with."

@schimekstudios

PILLOW TALK

Serve in a chilled coupe. Shake hard with ice and strain.

1 oz Pillow Talk Syrup
3 oz fresh pineapple juice
0.75 oz fresh lemon juice

Garnish with a pineapple fan.

Pillow Talk Syrup
Good for two weeks in the fridge, enough for 15 cocktails.
Bring 12 oz of water to a boil. Add water to 2 tsp of lapsang souchong loose tea; steep four minutes, then strain out solids. Avoid pressing the solids when straining otherwise the resulting liquid will be too tannic. Measure the liquid and add an equal amount of granulated sugar and 5 drops vanilla emulsion. Stir until dissolved.

DARYL SCHWARTZ | GOOD + BAR

"I think this secret sauce is not the drinks, it's about empowering people to socialize without the need for imbibing," states Daryl Schwartz on the Good + Bar mission.

A functional drink offers a choose-your-own-adventure approach to NA beverages. How do you want to feel? Whether the libation helps regulate your stress, declutters the mind, or induces a slight buzz, functional cocktails at Good + Bar are created with plant-based herbs to benefit the experience.

The idea started in 2018 when Schwartz hit a point where he was tired of drinking and developed the concept of functional NA cocktails and bars. "I must have been asleep for three years," he explains. "I woke up and there were 250 spirit brands in the market. I said to myself, now is the time to execute this concept."

Schwartz is the founder of Good + Bar (pronounced Good Bar) and specializes in NA activations, influencer events, and corporate gatherings. "If you create the environment for people, the brand experience, they connect in a way that's deeper and more meaningful," expresses Schwartz.

Schwartz imagines a future where "hopefully alcohol falls out of favor, like it is with the younger demographics; a point where more people take a load off by enjoying a drink that provides relaxation without being destructive or harmful. I think those winners are the people who figure out how to tap into their purpose for drinking, why they do it, and choose the functional option."

@drinkgoodbar

FIVE SPICE PAPER PLANE

Serve in a chilled coupe. Shake with ice and double strain.

2 oz DrZeroZero AmarNo
1.5 oz NA whiskey
0.75 oz blood orange-raspberry syrup*
0.5 oz fresh lemon juice
6 drops salt tincture*

Top with 2 oz Five Spice Macadamia Oat Foam*.
Garnish with coarse sea salt and a fresh raspberry.

*See page 42 Preparation Recipes.

BRYNN SMITH | BAR NEXT DOOR

"I have always had a natural inclination to be a little mixer," states Brynn Smith. "As a witch behind the bar, I grew up on a farm and would pick flowers to make perfumes. I loved to smell, and work with my hands. It was kismet when I started mixing and creating flavors."

"I fell in love with making drinks," expresses Smith, recalling the opportunity to attend a prestigious eight-week classic cocktail training course. Since then, she has run bar programs all over the city. "At Sotto, before all these beautiful AF products came out, I would make NA drinks for patrons, who then felt a part of the party and not just passed over with a cheeky club soda and a dash of whatever."

Bar Next Door, a cross-pollination of Art Deco, Rock-n-Roll, and Old Hollywood, is a love letter to the Sunset Strip. This is where we find Smith today as bar director. "All my cocktails are named after iconic locations, side streets, music venues, and hotels."

With approximately two percent of beverage orders NA drinks, Smiths' approach is to offer an AF twist on a classic. "The challenge with an aromatic drink like the Manhattan is getting the texture and viscosity, which is where the Luxardo Cherry syrup comes into play." A hospitality natural Smith states, "I love offering zero-proof options and seeing how it excites the NA community."

@bartendingpretty

MANHATTAN

Serve in a chilled nick and nora glass. Stir with ice and strain.

2 oz Lyre's American Malt
0.5 oz Ritual Zero Proof Aperitif Alternative
0.25 oz Luxardo Maraschino Cherries syrup
2 droppers All The Bitter Aromatic Bitters

Garnish with a skewered Luxardo Maraschino Cherry.

PREPARATION RECIPES

ACIDIFIED GRAPEFRUIT

Good for two days in the fridge, yields appx. 7.5 oz.

Combine 7.5 oz grapefruit juice with 1.5 tsp citric acid and whisk until citric acid is dissolved.

AGAVE SYRUP

Good for two weeks in the fridge, yields appx. 11 oz.

Combine 1 cup of agave nectar with 0.5 cup of hot water and stir until homogeneous.

ALOE HERB SPIRIT

Good for one month in fridge, yields appx. 12 oz.

Fill a pot with 3 cups of water. Chop aloe leaf into 1 cup of large pieces. Split the pieces in half and scrape the gel into the water, then add the outer leaf. Gather 1 cup of herb remnants, such as stalks from mint, the wooden part of rosemary, or any herbs you have in abundance. Boil the contents of your pot, stirring occasionally, until the liquid is reduced by half. Let mixture cool, then fine strain. The final liquid will have a reddish hue from the aloe gel.

BEET SYRUP

Good for two weeks in the fridge, yields appx. 3 oz.

Clean and cut one beet into chunks. Juice or blend until smooth, then pour through a fine mesh strainer. Combine juice with an equal quantity of sugar, stir until sugar is dissolved.

BLACKBERRY BALSAMIC SHRUB

Good for two weeks in the fridge, yields appx. 12-14 oz.

Crush 6 oz of blackberries into 8 oz demerara sugar, 2 oz water, and 1 oz balsamic vinegar. Cover and keep in the fridge for 24 hours, then pour through a fine mesh strainer. Rest in a sealed container in the fridge for five days.

BLOOD ORANGE RASPBERRY SYRUP

Good for two weeks in the fridge, yields appx. 2.5 cups.

Combine 1.5 cups fresh squeezed blood orange juice, 1 cup fresh raspberries, and 2 cups sugar in a small saucepan. Heat to a slow boil, stirring constantly. Reduce heat to low and simmer for five minutes. Remove from heat and rest to room temperature. Strain out the solids, pressing the contents through a fine mesh strainer.

ONCE UPON A COCKTAIL

CITRIC ACID SOLUTION

Will keep indefinitely, enough for lots of cocktails.

Whisk 3.5 oz of water with 3 tsp kosher salt until salt is dissolved.

CITRUS SALT

Good for three months at room temperature, enough for at least ten cocktails.

In a small bowl combine 2 tbsp pink himalayan sea salt with the zest of one lime. Mix together with fingers. Let dry completely then store in an airtight container.

DEMERARA SYRUP

Good for two weeks in the fridge, yields appx. 10 oz.

Combine 1 cup demerara sugar with 1 cup of water in a pan. Bring to a simmer and stir until sugar is dissolved.

FIVE SPICE MACADAMIA OAT FOAM

Good for one week in the fridge, yields appx 12 oz of foam.

Combine 0.5 cup macadamia milk, 0.5 cup oat milk, 1 tsp five-spice powder, 2 tbsp simple syrup, and 0.5 tsp vanilla emulsion in a blender and mix until smooth. Pour through a fine mesh strainer to remove any undissolved particles.

Transfer to a whipped cream canister, secure the top and charge with one nitrous oxide cartridge. Shake the canister vigorously for 20-30 seconds, then refrigerate for at least 30 minutes before dispensing.

PINEAPPLE SYRUP

Good for two weeks in the fridge, yields appx. 30 oz.

Remove skin and cut a quarter of a pineapple into chunks. Put through a juicer or blend until smooth, then pour through a fine mesh strainer. Combine juice with an equal quantity of sugar, stir until sugar is dissolved.

SALT TINCTURE

Will keep indefinitely, enough for lots of cocktails.

Mix 3.5 oz of water with 3 tsp kosher salt until salt is dissolved.

AWARD-WINNING CREATIVE
CUSTOM ART & BESPOKE WALLPAPER

Welcome to the BrightSide™

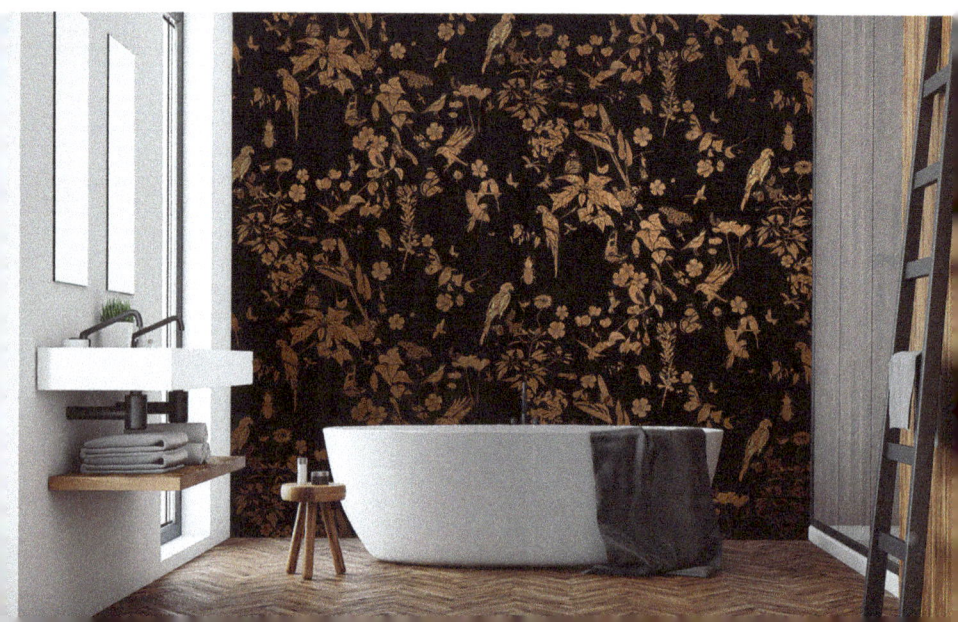

INQUIRE FOR YOUR DESIGN ONLINE

Salute to Sexy Sober Living
We Create Sexy Lounges for your Enjoyment

THE THIRD DEGREE
Hospitality Furniture

THE DRINK YOU DRINK WHEN YOU'RE NOT DRINKING

YOUR SIGNATURE MOCKTAIL DESERVES SIGNATURE GEAR.

BARFLY
— MIXOLOGY GEAR —

#BARFLYBYMERCER

AFTERWORD

To date, famous NA drinks would include an Arnold Palmer or a Shirley Temple. They have their place; however, we are exploring more dynamic creations in the NA movement. What they do have is mainstream accessibility, so world-wide bartenders know their build. These drinks should taste the same whether in Dubai or an outback bar in Australia.

The liquor world has over a century of documented cocktail recipes. Those libations have been made in households across every nook and cranny of the planet. The NA movement is so contemporary, there are no AF new-classic cocktails. We say "new-classics" as we don't want to confuse zero-proof interpretations, like an NA Margarita. How thrilling it is to be on the cusp of adventure looking for that standardized "new-classic." We imagine a person in Swindon, UK, may order that "new-classic" as easily as a person in West Hollywood, USA. And it should be built with similar ingredients and AF spirits, just as the creator intended.

As we draw a close on the *Once Upon a Cocktail - The LA Guide to the Non-Alcoholic Movement*, we believe we have only just begun to unearth the stories behind this new spirit category. Since we started out, we have met so many more brands and spokespeople in this arena. It would be a shame to stop the narration now. We simply conclude this movement needs a guidebook part-two. We even believe the dream-makers and booze-less shakers might need a documentary, and that pitch has been written... Watch this space; there is definitely more to come!

onceuponacocktail.world

WELCOME TO THE BRIGHTSIDE

Welcome to the Brightside, a creative agency, is the brainchild of international illustrator, artist, and designer Katie Brightside. The company is impassioned with a melting pot of creatives from vast spectrums of the arts and delivers unique design and artistic projects including this publication. The firm also houses *The Digs Collection*, a homeware company highlighting illustrated mural scale artwork, wallpaper, and handmade kimonos.

Brightside has secured several public art installations and personally received a WeHo Artist Grant, was an honoree of the Phyllis Morris Women in Leadership Award for Design and Entrepreneurship, and the John Chase accolade for Innovation of Art and Design at West Hollywood's Creative Business Awards.

Today, Brightside defies creative boundaries as the imagineer, author and illustrator of BBA'S 2024 Regional Cookbook award-winning *Once Upon a Cocktail – West Hollywood*, a recipe book featuring 54 most cherished venues across the city. Brightside is also a contributing illustrator for *Edible LA* and heads-up the magazine's cocktail column, "Drink Me" every quarter.

Graduating with a BA in fashion at Kingston University, UK, 2001, Brightside moved to Treviso, Italy, where she worked as a designer at United Colours of Benetton. In 2002 she relocated to Sydney, Australia. In 2012, the aMBUSH Gallery hosted her first of many solo art exhibitions. This successful exhibition inspired a thirst for further education, a MA Fine Art from Central Saint Martin (CSM), London. After graduation Brightside sought advice from a White Witch, asking where she would live happily-ever-after. A week later Katie fulfilled that prophecy by moving to West Hollywood.

welcometothebrightside.com

Printed in the USA
CPSIA information can be obtained
at www.ICGtesting.com
CBHW060749201124
17649CB00044B/1054